MOUNT VESUVIUS IN EIGHT FRAMES

WORKS BY SUDEEP SEN

POETRY

The Lunar Visitations
Kali in Ottava Rima
New York Times
Parallel
South African Woodcut
Mount Vesuvius in Eight Frames
Dali's Twisted Hands

FILM

Woman of a Thousand Fires
Babylon is Dying: Diary of Third Street
(WITH SUBHRA & JAYABRATO CHATTERJEE)
Kya Baat Hai
Cry Freedom
Colour My World

MOUNT VESUVIUS
in
EIGHT FRAMES

poetry by
SUDEEP SEN

etchings by
PETER STANDEN

WHITE SWAN BOOKS MISSOURI NEW YORK
PEEPAL TREE BOOKS LEEDS LONDON

Published by
Peepal Tree Books, 17 King's Avenue, Leeds LS6 1QS
White Swan Books, 919 Cathedral Station, New York, NY 10025

Author Photo by Rodney Prynne
Artist Photo by Stephen Katz

British Library Cataloguing in Publication Data
Sen, Sudeep, 1964-
Mount Vesuvius in Eight Frames
I. Title
821'.9'14

ISBN 0 948833 91 2

First Edition
Printed in Great Britain

for
my lovers, and true friends,
who must remain, unnamed.

ACKNOWLEDGEMENTS

'Mount Vesuvius in Eight Frames' was completed during my tenure as an invited visiting writer at the Open University 1994 Summer School at University of York.

I would especially like to express my gratitude to Dennis Walder, Cicely Havely, and Richard Allen, as well as, Lynda Prescott, Judith Palmer, and my writer colleagues, Jack Mapanje and Amyrl Johnson.

'Pompeian Idyll', the eight-etching series, by Peter Standen has been published earlier by Abacus as a postcard in 1980.

For their astute critical and editorial insight, I thank Jeremy Poynting and Mario Relich.

CONTENTS

Prologue / 11
Part 1 / 13
Plate 1 / 14
Part 2 / 15
Plate 2 / 16
Plate 3 / 18
Part 3 / 19
Plate 4 / 20
Part 4 / 21
Plate 5 / 22
Plate 6 / 24
Plate 7 / 26
Part 5 / 27
Part 6 / 29
Plate 8 / 30
Part 7 / 31
Part 8 / 32
Epilogue / 34

Suddenly the clouds detonate, and all the petals,
translucent, wet, coalesce: a blossoming mushroom,
peeling softly in a huge slow motion.
            s.s., 'Remembering Hiroshima Tonight'

An unannounced eruption reveals lilac
through the cracking skin of a dormant volcano
            s.s., 'Rivers of Fire'

MOUNT VESUVIUS IN EIGHT FRAMES

Prologue

Death has an invisible presence
  in the Vesuvian valley, even the corpses

bear an insidious resemblance, that belie
  shifting shadows in the subterranean alley.

Death has an invisible presence,
  so does life, in its incipience and its ends,

linked, like two inverted arches, bent
  to meet in a circle at their ends.

Strips of zinc, metal coated in wax,
bathed in acid, are scratched.

Year's twelve seasons reduced to eight --
the image slowly unfolds its fate

in the half-light, under transparent
protection of paper, moist and permanent,

etching the once-flowing blood stream,
now frozen as rich loam, ribbed lava reams.

1

But the story began long ago: Remember
   the young couple, together

starting their life, their dream home
   distilled from that embryo's yolk.

The sight chosen, the view determined —
   Mount Vesuvius -- this centrepiece

to be framed by an arched window pane
   of the bedroom's intimacy, and space.

2

Their house started breathing, piecing
itself at night -- the slow cementing

of bricks, supports, and the arch.
The building, traces its curve, its arms

locking tension in place. The spade
like a magical brush made

everything circulate, outlining
the movements, the inhabiting

16

of specific spaces, and the furniture's
  place. In a grand overture

the wooden bed with curved ends
  was placed right beneath the rails

of the window, overseen by Vesuvius.
  'Lava God!' they prayed, 'Bless us,

our love, and our curse.' The union of
  flesh, blood, smoke, and bones.

18

3

That evening unfolded naturally
and quietly, as deceptively

as the view's receeding perspective
drew them to the mountain peak —

to its air, the snow, its dust and fire.
Fire engulfed their bodies, their

fingers, burning nail-tips, furrowing
lines of passion on each other's skins.

4

It was freezing. The flames, frozen
  like tense icicles -- hard-edged,

brittle, tentative, chilled, eager.
  The night brought a strange winter.

That night there was black rain,
  everywhere -- nowhere to escape,

except amongst the synovial spaces
  of their intertwined limbs, as

their bodies remained locked in fear
and in death, around each other.

A marriage made in heaven, and in hell
buried unknowingly — skeletal

remains transfixed in the passion of
the very first night, unaware of

the world's changed face
and the undone terrain,

now completely re-done, different --
  calcified, stripped, eroded, irreverent --

the bright skies sheltering the ruins,
  the dark soil protecting the fossils.

Death has an invisible presence
  in the Vesuvian valley, even the corpses

bear an insidious resemblance, that belie
  shifting shadows in the subterranean alley.

5

Years later, two grave-diggers (or
archeologists, or conservationists, or

restorationists), stumbled, quite
by chance, upon this ancient site,

searching for something else,
following a geological trail —

a chameleon path of buried ash —
remains of civilisation, now washed.

Work began: Digging into the skin
  of the earth, defacing the soil, its

texture gradually ground further,
  reducing the grains finer and deeper.

Then liquid was poured, funnelling
  the volcanic shaft, clearing

the debris of the past
  itself, to unearth the past.

6

Then, a violent tremor, the plates
shifted, skies darkened, there was rain,

heavy rain -- a rain of redemption, healing
the lepered limbs, slowly washing

the bones to the last brittle and grain.
Death has an invisible presence

in the Vesuvian valley, even corpses
bear peculiar insidious resemblance.

7

Now, people come in great numbers, pay
  to see the same space --

the house, the room, that bed,
  the couple mummified as they last slept,

left unmoved, untouched, unaged.
  Mount Vesuvius still guard their gate

and the view -- the outside
  of the past, and the life, inside.

8

The dead: All neatly packed
in small square groups, and

in even multiples of eight,
nailed, framed, and glass-encased.

Even the new grave-diggers pay,
the elderly mountain pays

too -- in twos, fours, and eights.
Pompeii remains, uncontained.

Strips of zinc, metal coated in wax,
  bathed in acid, now re-scratched.

Year's twelve seasons reduced to eight --
  the image slowly unfolding its fate

in the half-light, under transparent
  protection of paper, moist and permanent,

etching the flowing blood stream, life
  frozen, yet unfrozen, rich lava, alive.

Epilogue

Death has an invisible presence
in the Vesuvian valley, even the corpses

bear an insidious resemblance, that belie
shifting shadows, in the subterranean alley.

Death has an invisible presence,
so does life, in its incipience and its ends,

linked, like two inverted arches, bent
to meet in a circle at their ends.

THE AUTHOR

SUDEEP SEN was born in New Delhi in 1964. He read at St. Columba's School and received his BA (HONOURS) in English Literature from the University of Delhi. He was an International Scholar at Davidson College, received an MA in Literature & Writing from Hollins College, and as an Inlaks Scholar he completed an MS from the Graduate School of Journalism at Columbia University in New York.

His first documentary film *Babylon is Dying* was nominated for the American Academy of Television Arts & Sciences Student Emmy Award. Since then, he has made four more films, including a seven-part television serial.

Sen's poetry collections include: *The Lunar Visitations, Kali in Ottava Rima, New York Times, Parallel, South African Woodcut,* and, *Mount Vesuvius in Eight Frames. Dali's Twisted Hands* is forthcoming later this year.

His numerous grants and awards include: the Faber & Faber poetry grant from the Arvon Foundation in the UK; the Bread Loaf Writers Conference Scholarship and the Vereen Bell Runner-Up Award in the USA; and, the Runners-Up Award in the British Council/Poetry Society of India National Poetry Competition.

His writings have appeared in the UK, USA, and India in leading newspapers and magazines including: *Times Literary Supplement, London Magazine, Poetry Review, The Scotsman, Boulevard, Poetry, The Times of India, The Illustrated Weekly of India, The Telegraph, The Independent, The Statesman & Society,* and broadcast on *BBC, SABC, AIR,* amongst others.

During the winter of 1992/93, he was the international poet-in-residence at The Scottish Poetry Library in Edinburgh.

Sen works as a writer, critic, and literary editor. He is at work on his next two collections, *April's Air* and *Blue Nude*. He divides his professional life between London and New Delhi.

THE ARTIST

PETER STANDEN was born in Carlshalton, Surrey, in 1936. He studied at Nottingham College of Art and Craft from 1954-56, and was awarded an Andrew Grant Open Bequest in 1956. He completed both his undergraduate and postgraduate studies from Edinburgh College of Art.

After two years (1960-62) of National Service with the British Army of the Rhine, he travelled extensively to Spain, North Africa, East Africa, Sudan, and the Middle East.

He has taught art at various schools, and in 1987 was the Scottish Arts Council Artist-in-Industry with Ferranti Professional Components plc in Dundee.

Standen has given several solo exhibitions ('Up the Nile', 'Paintings', 'Prints', 'Meet Mr Cat Lithographs', 'Back to the Future') and has been a part of various group shows ('Art into Landscape I and II', 'Five Scottish Printmakers', 'Biennale of Graphic Art', '21 X 21', 'International Graphic Exhibition', 'Inverclyde Biennale', 'Chessel Group', 'Morrison Portrait Competition', 'SSA Centenary Exhibition', 'An Edinburgh Suite', 'Fruitmarket Open', 'Grease and Water', 'Eight Artists') in Edinburgh, Dundee, London, Ljubjana, and Catania.

His work is part of a diverse collection, some of which include: Sautter-Fischbaker, Zurich; Hamilton Art Gallery, Ontario; Instituto Perla Cultura & L'Arte Catania, Scottish Arts Council; City Art Centre, Edinburgh; Leeds Education Department; International Club, London; Ferranti, Dalkeith and Dundee; and, Royal Bank of Scotland.

He has been member of The Edinburgh Printmakers Workshop since 1972, and of the Society of The Scottish Artists from 1965.

Currently, a documentary film is being made on his work. Standen lives and works in Edinburgh.

The text of 'Mount Vesuvius in Eight Frames'
is set in 10 point Omega typeface.
Each original plate of the eight-etching series
'Pompeian Idyll' measure 4" X 4".